Cla...

Here's to crun...

future you want to see.

Thank you for your

friendship + support. I'm

looking fwd to working

together this year!

A very special "Thank You!" to my friend, the brilliant <u>Mark Levy</u>, for summing up the message of this book when he said,

"The reality is, most people are living by some other guy's idea of what their future should be."

And, a very special "THANK YOU!" to the brilliant <u>Joel Bower</u>, who pushed me to write this book and create the corresponding courses that give readers and students a way to quickly apply and master the skills discussed herein.

This book is dedicated to....

My AMAZING wife Leanne, my partner in life and in business, who is as much as, if not more, responsible for the writing of this book and the design of *The Future 3 Skills: Builder Course Series*.

THANK YOU!

HOW TO STOP LIVING BY SOME OTHER GUY'S IDEA OF THE FUTURE AND START CREATING THE FUTURE YOU WANT TO SEE.

THE 3 SKILLS
YOU MUST HAVE
TO CREATE THE FUTURE
YOU
WANT TO SEE

BY JARED NICHOLS

THE NEWFUTURIST
Empowering PEOPLE to Shape The Future

ISBN-13: 978-0-9885821-7-0

Table of Contents

Dear Reader,

This book was written with YOU in mind. Yes, I know that sounds like the "right" thing to say to someone who has just purchased your book BUT…

it's the truth. What I mean is that so much of the material that is written today, material that's designed to help YOU navigate an uncertain future, is actually written with the author in mind.

I know because I've done this in the past without fully realizing it. The ideas, tools, and methods from some of my earlier writings were starting you out where I thought you should be, and not where you actually are today.

And that is why I wrote this book. It's short, simple, and immediately applicable to YOU, no matter who you are or what your occupation may be. You do not have to hold an advanced degree to understand and apply the concepts and strategies I share in this book.

At the end of each chapter, you'll find a call to action, to incorporate the seven habits of each skill into your daily life. I encourage you to keep a journal, or some place that you can write down your reflections from each chapter and how it applies to you.

I am excited that you've taken the first steps to creating the kind of future that you want to see. I honor you for that, and I'm delighted to join you on this journey.

To YOUR future success,

Jared Nichols | thenewfuturist.com
Founder, The Foresight Academy
Faculty Member, Haslam College of Business, University of Tennessee

Whose Idea of the Future Are YOU Creating?

This is one of the most important questions you can ask yourself today. It is a question that all of our futures depend on, because what we believe is possible determines the decisions we make and the future we create. And, most people, including many leaders, base their biggest decisions on someone else's idea of the future. They essentially allow some other guy to determine what is possible for them and their future. So, who is this "other guy" and why do so many people listen to him?

He, or she, is anyone we believe to be more knowledgeable, more confident, and more certain about the future than we are. It is someone we can easily outsource our thinking to in the midst of an increasingly chaotic and uncertain world. This other guy is not so much a single person as an amalgam of the loudest and surest voices in our world. It is the people we assume have it all figured out, either because they have achieved some level of success in the past or because they are just so brazenly confident going forward.

Whoever they are, their ideas are going to reflect in some way their own personal bias, beliefs, and desires. And while they may be incredibly knowledgeable in some areas, knowledge can only tell us about what is known. And the future is anything but.

So, regardless of who this "other guy" is and what his intentions are, his interpretation of the future is just an interpretation. And when you allow it to shape your whole outlook, it can undermine the potential you have to create an alternative outcome. It can lead you to sacrifice your imagination and creative potential in exchange for a false sense of security. Because whatever comfort this other guy's idea of the future may bring you, it is based on the false premise that the future is set is stone.

No one can tell us what to expect from a future that is still undecided, a future that relies so heavily on every action we do or don't take from this point forward. So, the best thing we can do right now is to enter into that uncertainty. To give ourselves the space we need to forget everything we think we know about the future, and to begin to reimagine it for what it could be. No one, and certainly not this "other guy," can predict what YOU are capable of. Whoever this "other guy" has been in your life, now is the time to remove the limitations they have placed on your future and rediscover your true potential.

I challenge you today to stop looking to the experts, the analysts, and futurists, like me, to tell you WHAT to think about the future. I have no desire to be one more talking head in your life. My desire is not tell you WHAT to think about the future, but to help you learn HOW to think about a future that is full of possibilities and anything but certain.

The future is far from a set destination, and those who will have the biggest impact take advantage of this fact each and every day. These people know if you view the future as something to prepare for, you miss your opportunity to create it. So, they take note of what the experts are saying, but then they ask, "What else is possible?"

They understand that nothing about the future is inevitable, and everything you do or don't do today will determine what that future looks like. They are not satisfied to just sit back and prepare for some other guy's idea of the future. They dare to envision something better, and believe in their ability to make it happen.

If you want a better future than the one being projected, then this has to be your focus as well. You have to stop preparing for some other guy's idea of the future and start creating your own.

> *You have to stop preparing for some other guy's idea of the future and start creating your own.*

Protect and Maintain Vs. Growth and Transformation

There are two kind of mentalities when it comes to thinking about the future. The first is what I call the "protect and maintain" mentality. The primary goal here is to avoid disruption, and maintain as much as possible what is comfortable and familiar. In other words, this approach works to maintain status quo. This strategy can only be successful for so long, because the one thing about the future that is certain is that it is going to be different than our current reality.

> *...the one thing about the future that is certain is that it is going to be different than our current reality.*

The people who are creating the future have a different kind of mindset. They look at the future as an opportunity for growth and transformation. The future they see is not a set of predictions and forecasts, but a vast ocean of possibility. They know if you are busy trying to protect the way you currently do things, you are going to miss your opportunity to do something better.

Because you are reading this book, I think it is safe to assume you want to be like this second group of people, those who refuse to prepare for some other guy's idea of the future, and who are boldly pursuing their own.

The three skills you will learn in this book are going to help you get there, and they are:

1. Expanding Your Awareness
2. Reimagining What is Possible
3. Creating New Realities

What Do These 3 Skills Achieve?

The first skill, *Expanding Your Awareness*, will help you see the true forces at work shaping the world. This skill will help you understand how your relationship to information and the narratives that define your world can keep you from seeing and fulfilling your true potential. As you become more aware of the external and internal forces guiding your future, you will learn to reassert control over the direction you are heading.

The next skill, *Reimagining What is Possible*, will help you see how vast and uncertain the future is, and how to use uncertainty to your advantage. This skill helps you explore a great variety of possible futures and connect your actions today to the future you want to see.

The final skill, *Creating New Realities*, will help you achieve a new vision for tomorrow, one that will inform your actions today and going forward. You will learn the most important elements of a powerful vision and how to ensure your actions today are taking you there and NOT toward some other guy's idea of the future.

These three skills together will start you an a path toward a future of YOUR choosing, instead of being stuck behind preparing for someone else's. If you want to stop avoiding disruption and start causing it, if you want to move from protecting and maintaining to growth and transformation, if you want to stop PREPARING for the future and start CREATING it, then read on my friend, and start creating the future on your terms.

Chapter 1: Expanding Your Awareness

When it comes to creating the kind of future you want to see, your chances of success depend on your ability to recognize the forces shaping your future, so you can begin influencing and using them to your advantage. That is why this is the first skill on the list. Once you become aware of who and what is creating tomorrow, you will understand the role you can play in creating the future you want to see. Expanding your awareness isn't just increasing your exposure to information.

Sometimes it involves limiting your exposure. It is about pulling back the curtain and identifying the forces at work behind the information.

The Hidden Power of Narratives

Expanding your awareness begins by learning to recognize the narratives behind the information we receive, whether it's from the media or from our own brains. These are the stories that give life and meaning to the information we consume. They determine how we interpret the information and how that interpretation impacts our thoughts and actions, ultimately determining the future we create.

We have to identify and closely examine these narratives, so we can determine if they are the stories we want shaping tomorrow.

- *Whose idea of the future do they represent?*
- *What do they say is possible or desirable for our future?*
- *How do they define the role we play in creating it?*

These are the questions we must ask ourselves if we are going to recognize the power these narratives have in our lives. Only then can we begin to take ownership of the stories that define us and our future.

You see, stories have a real power and impact in our lives. They are how we make sense of the world. They form the basis of our relationships to each other, and, how we understand and communicate with other people. They determine what we can come to expect and depend on each other for. They can create unity around a shared set of ideas and principles. And, they can inspire and motivate us toward a common cause.

You can probably think of some stories right now that define your family, your business, your community, or your country. Maybe you have a narrative in your family around a particular character trait, like honesty, for instance. You remind your children often of the virtues of honesty and warn them against dishonest people. They grow to believe that being honest first, regardless of the consequences, is the best way to achieve the kind of success in life that matters.

This narrative that honesty will lead them toward a happy and fulfilled life then guides their decisions and their actions going forward. It may help them determine who they will marry or help them avoid a potentially disastrous relationship. It could influence the kind of work they do or the manner in which they do it.

The consequences of this narrative, if they integrate it into their lives, could have far reaching implications for their future. But, there's a good chance that this child is not even aware of the narrative and how it guides them on a daily basis. They might not take the time to examine why they choose to avoid certain people or why certain actions don't sit right with them. The story about honesty registers more as a feeling they have about the world and the information they receive from it. This feeling then translates into decisions and actions that ultimately determine the course of their future.

This is how narratives work. They enable you to quickly make judgments without analysis. And this can be helpful sometimes, but not all the narratives that penetrate our lives have such positive outcomes. Some we wouldn't choose for ourselves at all. They are simply the ones we've been given because they permeate our society and our culture. We usually don't see these stories as "stories." We just accept them as the way things are. And this can be dangerous for our future. If we don't realize these narratives exist, then we can't challenge them. When we don't challenge them, we run the risk of allowing a false narrative to decide our future for us.

> *If we don't realize these narratives exist, then we can't challenge them. When we don't challenge them, we run the risk of allowing a false narrative to decide our future for us.*

So, the first step to expanding your awareness is identifying the narratives at work in your life. Do they reflect who it is you want to be or are they based on some other guy's idea of what is possible for you and your future? If you can stay aware of these narratives and challenge them on a regular basis, you will be able to remove the ones that aren't leading to the future YOU want to create.

Your Relationship to Information

Maintaining our focus is one of the biggest challenges we face in the world today. Distractions come from every direction on a near constant basis. It is hard to discern what deserves our attention and for how long, and it is even harder to determine what we should make of all the information we receive. That's why expanding your awareness must involve recognizing the impact of media in your life and understanding how your relationship to information affects your ability to create the future.

Why is this so important? Because the sad reality is we tend to lose all intention and purpose when we pick up our personal information devices, which are no longer just "phones." While these devices are central to our ability to communicate, to learn, and to stay current, they are also our kryptonite. They tend to assert more control over us than we do over them. We allow them to tell us what deserves our attention, which happens to be everything, all the time. As a result, we don't know where to focus, and we lose our ability to maintain momentum and make an impact where it really matters. Our focus is central to our ability to create the future.

> *Our focus is central to our ability to create the future.*

We cannot afford to move forward mindlessly and allow distractions to rob us of our attention and our intention. We must change our relationship to information. We have to make information work for us and not the other way around.

This starts by understanding the arrangement by which we receive our information. As Apple's CEO Tim Cook once famously said,

"When the service is free, YOU are the product."

You have to understand that, the greatest factor in determining what information gets put in front of you is how likely you are to click on it.

> *…the greatest factor in determining what information gets put in front of you is how likely you are to click on it.*

They know your tastes. They know your preferences. And most of all, they know how to distract you. This can sometimes work in your favor, but let's face it, not all of us have the greatest track record in this department. Don't perpetuate this self-reinforcing feedback loop of distraction by continuing to click on junk.

The important thing here is to overcome mindlessness and begin to exercise your intention again. YOU decide what deserves your attention, and learn to use information as a tool instead of allowing it to use you.

This is what I mean by your *relationship* to information. It is often an emotional thing, just like with narratives. It is based on an unconscious response to stimuli, one that is frequently unnoticed and unquestioned. The information is put in front of you, and you consume it, with little regard to whether it is good for you. Now that you understand this arrangement, you can begin to change this relationship.

I find it helps to think of information as food. I'm sure you've heard of the term "information diet." The truth is that our world today has a surplus of information, and most of it is not very good for you. In the last century, a similar phenomenon occurred with our access to food. We reached a place where we had more food than we needed, and we had to come to terms with the fact that most of it was junk. We are in the same situation today with media. So, you need to set your own guidelines now for healthy information consumption.

Here is how you can start:

- Know what matters most to you. Think long-term here. This is how you maintain your intention and don't fall prey to instant gratification.
- Use information as a tool, instead of allowing it to use you. You have more free access to knowledge than anyone in history. Use it wisely.
- Go beyond the major headlines and look to what is occurring on the fringes. This is where change comes from. If you pay attention to what's happening here, you can spot it early while there is time to be proactive. Again, use your interests (what matters most to you) as your guide here.

It's important to remember that you can't know everything about everything. Your goal here should be to know as much as you can about the things that matter most to you and to the future you want to create. If you can maintain your focus and your intention in today's world, you will have a tremendous advantage in creating the future you want to see. Begin changing your relationship to information today.

Rewriting Your Future

Once you are aware of how narratives and information impact your world and your future, you can begin to use them to your advantage. We just discussed how to do this with information. Let's focus now on how you can use the power of narrative to flip the script on your future.

You've already learned the importance of rooting out the narratives at work in your life. Challenging these narratives on a regular basis it the only way that you can take ownership of the stories guiding your future.

So, now I want you to focus on the big overarching narratives that define you. What role do you believe you should play in shaping the future? I am using the term "role" here, because we all have unwritten roles to play when it comes to our lives and our future. These are the ideas that we let define us and what we believe we can achieve. Again, these narratives are not always as obvious as we think they are, but even the obvious ones we too often fail to question.

Take, for example, the following illustration. A young entrepreneur is starting out in an emerging field. He finds himself in largely uncharted territory, so he begins to search for a model of success. He is looking for someone or something to follow, so that he can know what to expect and what is expected from him. He finds this model in the best-selling books of an older, highly successful entrepreneur, who is both sharp and a little flashy. While the young entrepreneur is not a fan of the older man's style, he follows him because he wants to ensure that he makes the right moves and impresses the right people. He buys into this man's narrative, so that he can achieve a similar level of success. He just wants to get it right so that the people who depend on him, such as his wife and kids, aren't let down.

After years of following this model and achieving a fair degree of success, the now not-so-young entrepreneur finds himself dissatisfied and unfulfilled. He feels like he did everything right, but something vital to maintaining his momentum is missing. It is only then that he begins to question his narrative. And when he does, he finds that his current definition of success, based on this other man's model, doesn't match what he really wants to achieve. It is not a reflection of his passion or his potential. And, it will never lead him to make his biggest impact on the future. So, he decides right then and there to redefine what success means to him. And, it starts with understanding the impact that he wants to make.

That younger entrepreneur was me, and the impact I wanted to make was helping MORE people learn how to think about the future. It was simple, but the model I was following was only going to help certain elite or well-financed individuals learn this skill set. That's when I decided to change my focus and my strategy and started on a path that has brought me here today.

This one decision changed not just the direction of my work, but so many other aspects of my life. It greatly increased my level of motivation, my sense of fulfillment, and my freedom from worrying about things that don't really matter to me or the future I want to create. I want the same for you. So, I want you to ask yourself the following questions:

- *How do I define success?*
- *Am I following someone else's model?*
- *Am I creating some other guy's idea of the future?*

I want you to be conscious of the role you are playing in creating the future. Has it been designed by you or someone else? The reason this is so important is because we each have a unique potential to fulfill, a unique purpose to serve. The future depends on you finding yours and defining for yourself the role you want to play. If you never question or take ownership of the narrative that defines you and the work you are doing in the world, you will never make your greatest contribution to the future.

> *If you never question or take ownership of the narrative that defines you and the work you are doing in the world, you will never make your greatest contribution to the future.*

You cannot allow someone else's ideas to limit your potential and the impact you are meant to make in the world. Now is the time to decide what you want that impact to be. You have to define what success means to you. This is how you rewrite the role you want to play and flip the script on your future.

How to Build This Skill in YOUR Life

Awareness isn't something you acquire, it has to be practiced and maintained. It is your new way of relating to the world and the information that it sends you. In order for you to maintain your focus and intention going forward, you must practice this skill on a regular basis.

Below are the key habits to build in order to maintain your awareness. Practicing these habits will be crucial to your success as you continue to navigate a world full of distractions. Remember, YOU have the power to shape the future, and these habits will help you make your biggest impact.

TAKE ACTION: Seven Habits for Expanding Your Awareness

1. IDENTIFY the narratives that are influencing your thoughts and decisions.
2. DISCARD false or unhelpful narratives on a regular basis.
3. USE information as a tool, instead of allowing it to use you.
4. LOOK beyond your normal range of vision to the fringes.
5. THINK long-term and avoid the constant draw of instant gratification.
6. DEFINE the role you want to play.
7. RECOGNIZE the power you have to shape the future.

The Actions I'll Take to Expand My Awareness Are:

_____

_____

_____

_____

_____

_____

_____

_____

_____

_____

_____

_____

_____

_____

Chapter 2: Reimagining What is Possible

If you want to create a better future, you need to build your ability to RE-imagine what's possible, not just for you, but for the future as a whole. This skill is critical when it comes to creating the future, because if we can't first imagine it, then we're never going to create it! So, forget everything you think you know about the future and begin to see the future anew, especially in terms of its broader potential.

The Future is Uncertain (And That's a Good Thing)

People come to me and others in my field because they are looking for a sense of certainty about the future. They need something that they can plan around and prepare for. What they find though, is that the future is anything but certain. But, as we begin to explore the future together, their desire for security is quickly replaced by their excitement about the possibilities.

The future suddenly becomes a lot bigger and their ability to impact it becomes a lot more real. The future is no longer about their ability to plan, but about their ability to create. This is the greatest benefit of reimagining what is possible. It is in realizing the extent to which those possibilities are up to you and what you are able to imagine. So, my message to you is, don't be afraid of an uncertain future. It may be your greatest opportunity.

> *Don't be afraid of an uncertain future. It may be your greatest opportunity.*

You can turn uncertainty into a strategic advantage, and it comes down to HOW you think about the future. Unfortunately, most people only want to know WHAT to think about the future.

Again, they are looking for certainty that they can plan around, so they allow some other guy's idea of the future to determine what is possible for them. Thinking about the future becomes an exercise in avoiding disruption, rather than looking for opportunities to *cause* disruption. Uncertainty is viewed as an obstacle to business as usual, rather than an opportunity to do things differently. Countless opportunities to create something better are missed in the process.

Reimagining what is possible requires that you take the opposite approach. It starts by recognizing that the future is first and foremost uncertain, and that it rests largely on your ability to create it. Futurists do, of course, consider probabilities and make forecasts, but these are by no means treated as certainties. They are merely opportunities for you to determine how you might take advantage of potential changes in order to reach your desired destination.

Again, this is the difference between the "protect and maintain" mentality and the "grow and transform" mentality. Your focus is not on how to protect what you're currently doing, but on how to transform it based on a broader idea of what is possible. You will not reach your desired destination if you view change as a threat to your current way of doing things.

> *You will not reach your desired destination if you view change as a threat to your current way of doing things.*

You have to embrace it as an opportunity to grow and transform in order to make a bigger impact. Again, you have to treat uncertainty as an asset, not a liability.

So, unless you are a big fan of the status quo, uncertainty is your friend. It is your opportunity to make things better. One thing that I say again and again to my clients and students is that, WHAT you think about the future is not as important as HOW you think about the future.

> "WHAT you think about the future is not as important as HOW you think about the future."

We look to the experts to tell us WHAT to think about the future, when our primary focus should be on HOW we are thinking about it. We need to build the skills necessary for thinking about the future in a more meaningful and productive way. That's why I wrote this book.

Thinking about the future in terms of uncertainty is one way to do this. When you are actively looking for the uncertainty around a forecast or prediction, you will discover the opportunity that exists to create an alternative outcome. Don't treat the future like a set destination.

> *Don't treat the future like a set destination.*

Allow yourself to appreciate the full spectrum of possibilities. Embracing uncertainty is how you open yourself up to these possibilities and begin to reimagine the future that YOU can create.

Context Is the Key

Context is the key to unlocking what is possible. This may sound strange, but let me explain. There are two reasons that context is so important. The first is that we can't understand the impact of future changes unless we consider them in the context of the future.

For instance, when we think of the impact that a new technology or potential event might have, we tend to imagine how it would impact us if it were here today. As a result, it's easy to get worked up about potential future issues or events like mass automation, universal healthcare, or cryptocurrencies. These kinds of issues can bring people a great deal of anxiety, as they imagine how our current institutions or systems might fall apart under the pressure of these kinds of changes. But, contextually speaking, they are failing to see the bigger picture of the future.

Because the future context is going to be different than our current context, the impacts and implications of these potential events will also be different than what we would see today.

If 47% of jobs go to automation in the next decade or two (as some predict), then that doesn't mean that 47% of people will be unemployed. The future context will be different. The nature of work will change. New fields will emerge. And, it is those who are able to anticipate this reality that will be in a position to take advantage of these possibilities.

> *It is those who are able to anticipate this reality that will be in a position to take advantage of these possibilities.*

They will be more likely to use these potential changes as opportunities to grow and transform. They will be able to reimagine the impact that they can make in terms of these greater possibilities. Context gives you that window into possible futures, and enhances your ability to see the fuller potential.

In fact, you can even use context as a tool for uncovering this kind of hidden potential, which is the second reason context is so vital to reimagining what is possible. Experts have a terrible track record at anticipating how a certain technology or trend will play out because they fail to consider the larger context. In the field of foresight, we refer to these trends and technologies as drivers, or driving forces.

Drivers have an unknown trajectory because their full potential is still emerging. They may have already had an impact in a specific area or industry, but their broader potential is still unknown. Again, context is the key to unlocking this unknown potential.

Take, for instance, the impact of genetic modification. We have already seen the impact of gene therapy in treating certain diseases, like specific kinds of cancer, but we have yet to realize its potential to eliminate disease through the genetic modification of future generations. We have also seen the use of genetic modification to increase crop yields or modify populations of disease-carrying mosquitoes, but we have yet to understand the full implications this kind of modification will have on the planet as we continue to apply it. The full social, political, and environmental implications of genetic modification are still anyone's guess.

Consider the following questions:

- *What will happen if we start to modify humans for intelligence, appearance, and certain physical attributes?*
- *What will happen if this technology is only accessible to the elite few with the means to afford it?*

- *If life-extending gene therapies dramatically increase longevity, how might a longer life redefine career trajectories, retirement, and what it means to grow old?*

All of this potential can be uncovered through the framework of context. It is here that you can discover a broader array of possible futures. And when you can reimagine the future in this way, you are much more likely to spot the opportunities to create the kind of the future you want to see.

So, when you are trying to understand how a certain trend or technology might impact the future, you must consider the broader context in which it will unfold. This includes the social, political, and environmental implications, to name a few. Reimagining what is possible requires that you go beyond what is here and now and consider the bigger picture of the future.

Reimagining YOUR Future

The biggest factor in determining what is possible for your future is YOU. You, and people like you, are the biggest reason that the future is so hard to predict. Because no one knows exactly what you will choose to do, the impact you will make, and what you will discover to be possible. Because of you, a multitude of futures currently exist. Once you understand this, you must apply it to your own life.

There is so much uncertainty right now in how the rest of your life will play out. In fact, there is even uncertainty in how the rest of your day will play out. Use it to your advantage. Do something unpredictable. You have the ability to imagine something, and then create it. You have the ability to do something that hasn't been done before. This is the benefit of reimagining what is possible. You begin to see how every action you do or don't take today determines what tomorrow may bring.

> *You begin to see how every action you do or don't take today determines what tomorrow may bring.*

Even the smallest of changes can start you on a trajectory toward an alternative future. It's as simple as determining what actions you can take today to start you on that alternate path toward a future of your choosing. We tend to think of powerful people and institutions as the arbiters of the future. We do the same when it comes to technology and scientific discovery. But, the very things we see as shaping the future and determining what is possible only hold the power that WE give them.

> *But, the very things we see as shaping the future and determining what is possible only hold the power that WE give them.*

Think about it. These entities, institutions, and technologies, didn't create themselves. WE created them. And because of that, it's our job to decide the role that they will play in creating a future of OUR choosing. As you continue to reimagine what is possible, don't forget the power you possess to create an alternative future.

This is how humanity has progressed and evolved throughout history. They imagined something better, something different, and they created it. It is our history and our nature as human beings. When you are reimagining what is possible, you are stepping into that tradition of unlocking this greater potential to the benefit of future generations.

How to Build This Skill in YOUR Life

Just like with the skill of expanding awareness, reimagining what is possible is an ongoing practice. It is your means of exploring the future and continuously discovering new territory and hidden potential.

Below are the key habits to build in order to continue reimagining the future. Practicing these habits will be crucial to your ability to recognize and take advantage of opportunities to create the kind of future you want to see. Remember, YOU have the power to shape the future, and these habits will help you make your biggest impact.

TAKE ACTION: Seven Habits for Reimagining What is Possible

1. SEE the future(s) as a spectrum of possibility rather than a single inevitability.
2. LOOK for the uncertainty around potential events.
3. USE uncertainty as an opportunity to create a different outcome.
4. CONSIDER how the future context might change.
5. USE context to uncover the hidden potential of drivers.
6. IDENTIFY how small changes can shift the trajectory.
7. UNDERSTAND that PEOPLE (like you) determine what is possible.

The Actions I'll Take to Reimagine What is Possible Are:

_____

_____

_____

_____

_____

_____

_____

_____

_____

_____

_____

_____

_____

_____

_____

_____

_____

Chapter 3: Creating New Realities

This third and final skill is where you learn to fully connect to the future you want to create. You put yourself there and experience it. Then, you bring that experience back to the present day so that other people can be a part of it. This is how you move others to action, both the people you want to serve and the people you will need to help you build this reality. This is also how you make the necessary changes to maintain the focus and drive you will need going forward. This is how new realities are created, and it all starts with a vision.

Where to Start

Earlier in this book I mentioned that the difference between how most people think about the future and reimagining what is possible, is that the former bases its strategy on what has worked in the past, while the latter bases its strategy on what is possible in the future.

If you want to continue on your same trajectory and maintain your current reality until something comes along to disrupt it, then base your strategy on what has worked in the past. But, if you want to create a new reality, you have to START in the future. The future is where true innovation comes from. In order to be truly innovative, you have to step outside of your current reality.

> *In order to be truly innovative, you have to step outside of your current reality.*

That means that you must forget about whatever it is that you currently do. You have to forget about how you currently serve your clients or communicate with your audience. You have to forget about the way you operate today and even the value that you currently provide. These are all subject to change when you are looking at the long-term future.

The benefit of starting in the future is that you are opening yourself up to that growth and transformation now while there's time to be proactive. You are going there first and seeing what value you can provide in that new reality.

If a new technology or trend is threatening to disrupt the way you currently do things, you can go beyond that for a moment. You can step into that future and see what opportunities it holds for you. The key to doing this successfully is that when you step into the future, you focus on the PEOPLE that you want to serve.

Ask yourself:

- *What might this new reality be like for them?*
- *How have their needs changed?*
- *In what new way can you enrich their lives?*

This is how you discover the new value you can provide. This is how you discover the transformation you must undergo in order to serve them better. This is how you begin to see the new reality that is waiting to be created.

This is the vital part of creating new realities that most people miss. They want to protect the way they currently do things, failing to consider if this is best for the people they serve. If you don't start in the future, you will miss these vital opportunities to grow and change and to make a bigger impact in their lives. Instead, you'll be stuck defending status quo and hoping to avoid disruption. That is the protect and maintain mentality. Starting in the future frees you from that.

So, in order to create a new and better reality, you must go to the future first and focus on what you can do there to improve the lives of the people you serve. This is how you discover a vision that is worth pursuing.

Moving Others to Action

Once you connect yourself to that future reality you want to create, you must learn to communicate this vision in way that moves others to action. We can learn a lot about moving others to action by looking at the famous visionary leaders from the past. What do these leaders have in common? They had a vision that was transformative and they put PEOPLE in the center of it.

Think of Martin Luther King, Jr.'s "I Have a Dream" speech. Why were so many people willing to risk their safety to follow him? It was because he was able to communicate his vision in a way that people could experience its transformative potential. They could imagine themselves in that new reality that they themselves had a hand in creating.

Why did we go to the moon in 1969? Because a very charismatic president named John F. Kennedy was able to convince the American people several years earlier that, against all odds, this would be their defining achievement. He gave them a transformative vision of the future that they could pursue. These men were great leaders not because they played it safe, but because they communicated a bold and compelling vision that people wanted to be a part of.

There are two things to remember when communicating your vision. The first is that you aren't afraid to be idealistic. Idealism is often avoided or scaled back because of fear of failure. If a goal seems unattainable, then the fear is that no one would pursue it. This is why it is so important to communicate a vision in a way that people are able to experience its transformative reality.

> *...communicate a vision in a way that people are able to experience its transformative reality.*

If the experience seems authentic and people can connect to it, then idealism becomes an asset rather than a flaw. Idealism, even against all odds, was not a concern for Kennedy or King, and that was because people were at the center of their visions.

That brings us to the second thing you must remember when communicating your vision, which is to engage the human element. Remember, the future is uncertain because we can't predict what people will do. Your vision must emphasize that this future reality is up to them and the actions they take today. The people themselves are the change-makers, the revolutionaries, the pioneers. You aren't creating this new reality, they are.

You are empowering them to take advantage of this opportunity to transform their lives. You see this everyday in very effective advertising campaigns. Take Apple's commercials, for example. They aren't about how great Apple products are. They are about the great things that PEOPLE can do when they use Apple products. These advertisements are full of idealism, but that transformative potential hinges on the people that are the center of that vision. This is how people are inspired and moved to creating that new reality.

So, if you want to move people to action, then you must put them in the center of a transformative reality that they can help create. That is how you communicate a vision worth pursuing.

Creating YOUR Future Today

While your vision has to inspire other people to action, YOU are the one who has to take the first steps. That begins with making the necessary changes in your life that will set you on your new course. Too many people overlook the necessity of creating alignment with their new vision. They fail to realize that everything they do today determines the reality they will create. Alignment is about setting your new trajectory and ensuring that every area of your life is on board. It's not enough to have a vision, you have to be able to connect your actions TODAY to that future reality.

> *It's not enough to have a vision, you have to be able to connect your actions TODAY to that future reality.*

That begins with aligning how you spend your time, your energy, and your money with your vision of the future. This can't be a surface level assessment. You will need to get deep and granular with each of these areas and decide what shifts need to occur to change your trajectory. Chances are you will find that many of your actions and priorities still have you on that old trajectory, leading to some other guy's idea of the future.

Before you start moving forward, make sure it is in the right direction. Alignment requires a high level of commitment, but if you're not willing to commit to your vision, then you can't expect anyone else to either. So, go ahead and make sure that your time, energy, and money are feeding your vision and not someone else's.

Once you are headed in the right direction, the next priority is to maintain momentum. That means you need to constantly be looking for the next step you can take to move your vision forward. Practicing the first two skills, by building your awareness and your ability to reimagine what is possible, will help you discover these next steps as you go. You have a level of focus now that only a strong vision can provide, when before, you may not have known where to look. When you know the reality you want to create, you are more likely to find the resources and the people you need to make it happen.

> *When you KNOW the reality you want to create, you are more likely to find the resources and the people you need to make it happen.*

When I decided that my vision was to help MORE people learn HOW to think about the future, it didn't take long for me to begin identifying the tools and the people that would support this vision. People are drawn to a powerful vision, especially in today's world where that level of clarity and commitment is hard to find.

Not only does your vision provide you with a level of focus that is hard to come by, it also provides you with an endless source of motivation. When you are working toward a long-term vision of the future, there will be times when you need to tap into the energy of that future reality. It helps to regularly step into the new reality that you are working so hard to create. Allow yourself to appreciate it and to be grateful for the opportunity you have today. This practice will help you reconnect your actions with your greater purpose and reignite your passion to make it happen.

How to Build This Skill in YOUR Life

While you will not be creating a new vision on a regular basis, certain habits will help you as you work to make that vision a reality. As I just mentioned, revisiting that vision often, will keep you focused and motivated, and that requires that you start in the future and focus on the impact you can make in other people's lives.

A vision is a message you will need to communicate again and again, and these habits will keep that message strong and on target. Altogether, these habits will help you maintain your direction and your momentum until that vision becomes a new reality.

TAKE ACTION: Seven Habits for Creating New Realities

1. START in the Future.
2. FOCUS on the people you want to serve.
3. EMBRACE idealism.
4. ENGAGE the human element.
5. ALIGN your life with your vision.
6. USE your vision as your source for motivation, to re-energize and renew.
7. TAKE the next step to always keep your vision moving forward.

The Actions I'll Take to Create New Realities Are:

_____

_____

_____

_____

_____

_____

_____

_____

_____

_____

_____

_____

_____

_____

_____

Going Forward...

Creating the future you want to see is no small feat. It takes time. It takes commitment. It takes a willingness to grow and transform as an individual first. And that transformation starts with small steps toward a bigger vision. My challenge to you is to go back to the seven habits under each skill and make them a routine practice in your daily life.

Each of these habits are designed to give you a quick win each and every day. The key of course, is to start. Start with one habit from one skill and work on that until it becomes second nature for you. Then, move on to the next.

You do NOT have to have it all figured out before you begin. Just get started and I promise you'll begin to see changes in various aspects of your life.

I know that sounds too good to be true, but I say this because I've seen it happen in the lives of many individuals. I've seen leaders of large organizations change the way they think about themselves and the opportunities they have to grow their company and improve the lives of the people they serve.

I've seen small business owners and entrepreneurs embrace uncertainty as a strategic advantage, and they no longer feel like they are constantly working to stay afloat. The difference for both of these groups is that they are truly being proactive about the future they want to see.

They are intentional about the actions they're taking today, because they know that the LEGACY they're creating is one they can truly be proud of. These individuals have mastered *The 3 Skills,* and I know, because I've had the privilege to work with them and watch them transform into the leaders they are today.

Seeing that on a consistent basis is why I created *The Future 3: Skills Builder Course Series.* This series is for those individuals who want to master *The 3 Skills* more quickly and with even greater confidence.

So, What is The Future 3: Skills Builder Series?

This series is broken down into three mini-courses, each designed to quickly accelerate your ability to make these three skills an ongoing practice in both your personal and professional lives. Each course is designed around one of *The 3 Skills* and dives deeper into the seven habits for mastering that skill on a daily basis.

Most important of all though is that each video in the course includes a challenge to put what you've learned to practice right away. This is what helps you achieve mastery more quickly, and that is why I'm so excited about this series.

The first course in the series is *The Awareness Builder*. This course helps you see the true forces at work shaping the world. We start by breaking down the two kinds of narratives that hold the most power over your life and how you can identify and break free from those that are not serving your greater aspirations.

Next, I'll teach you how to reframe your relationship to information and give you practical ways to move from information OVERWHELM to actionable INSIGHT. Then, I'll show you how to find your area of focus and put your time and energy into what matters most to you, because, it's here where you can make your greatest and most meaningful impact.

From there I will teach you how to spot early signs of change and disruption, giving you the ability to TRULY be proactive in the actions you take today.

The last video in this course is all about YOU and YOUR power and potential to shape and create the future that you want to see. It's here where you will see that the greatest moments of real change throughout human history occurred when PEOPLE like YOU decided to take action to make their vision of the future a reality.

The second course in this series is *The Re-imagination Builder*. This course helps you see just how vast and uncertain the future is, so you can learn how to use that uncertainty to your advantage. In this course, you will learn how to explore a variety of possible futures and connect your actions today to the future you want to see.

It's here that you learn how to create context for the future which is where the opportunities for REAL innovation truly exist. In this course I will also teach you how to uncover the hidden potential that emerging trends and drivers of change hold for the future, and what that means for YOU.

The third course is *The New Realities Builder.* This course is about achieving a new vision for tomorrow, and taking the actions needed today to make that vision a reality. You will learn the core attributes of a powerful vision and how to realign your life and actions toward it.

It's here that I'll teach you how to stand in the future and work backwards to determine the actions you need to take TODAY. I'll also show you how to align your life and work toward that vision of the future by helping you evaluate where you're spending your time, energy, and money, and determining if it's creating the future YOU want to see or someone else's.

The last part of this course is about how to move forward and make these skills and habits a consistent practice in your daily life, because learning something new is one thing, but mastering something new is completely different. And that is why this course and this entire series exists.

It's about YOU finding the insight, the clarity, and the focus you need to to actively create a better world. It's about YOU discovering the power you possess to take a more intentional and proactive role in determining what's possible for you and your future.

That's why I'm including this series as an added bonus and a "THANK YOU" for purchasing this book. The regular price for this series is $667, but I'm offering it to you for only $247. I TRULY want you to be successful in this endeavor, and because of that I offer you this challenge.

Join me in these courses and try it out for 30 days. Put the action steps I give you to the test, and if you feel like I don't deliver on my promise, then send me your work and I'll send you your money back. All of it.

The link to get your discount and access to the series is below. But, before I sign off, I want to leave you with this thought:

> *The future never arrives. It is always out in front of you, waiting to be created. So go create it!*

To get your bonus discount for purchasing this book, please visit: https:// www.theforesightacademy.com/offers/uHm6qDLt

About the Author

 Jared Nichols is a futurist, advisor, and faculty member at the University of Tennessee's Haslam College of Business, in Graduate and Executive Education. He is the founder of The Foresight Academy where he teaches leaders, teams, and individuals, how to think like futurists so they can create the best future possible, for themselves and the people they serve.

Jared hold's a Master's Degree in Strategic Foresight, and is sought out by leaders, organizations, and entrepreneurs to help them identify how emerging trends in technology, media, business, and public policy, may fundamentally change society and shape the future.

His insight and expertise is utilized across a wide variety of sectors and industries from Fortune 500 companies to government municipalities, entrepreneurial start-ups, as well as his work in Hollywood with accomplished actors, writers, and producers, helping them reinvent themselves and discover new areas for growth both inside and outside the bounds of their industry.

Jared is also the host of the small business podcast presented by the National Small Business Association titled, The Road Ahead: Small Business in the 21st Century, which focuses on practical tips and insights for small business owners on how to grow, thrive, and contribute, in a volatile and uncertain environment. In addition to hosting The Road Ahead, Jared also sits on the Board of Trustees for the National Small Business Association with a focus on equipping SME's with the ability to anticipate change and influence public policy in favor of small business growth.

Jared is the author of Rethinking Your Next Quarter (Century): How to Create Continuous Growth and Ensure Future Relevance, Rethinking Reinvention, Leading the 21st Century: The CEO's Guide to Thriving in a Volatile and Uncertain Future, and Four Futures for the 21st Century Non-Profit.

Jared is also a musician, composer, competitive cyclist, and trail runner living in Charlotte, North Carolina with his wife and their two sons.

His most recent accomplishment is becoming an official card carrying member of the Dollar Beard Club and he is already making plans to build a workshop and tame a wild animal.

How to Connect and Contact Jared:

For more information about Jared's work and The New Futurist, please visit: www.thenewfuturist.com

To contact Jared for customized work or to have Jared speak at your next event, please contact him directly at: jared@thenewfuturist.com

Connect with Jared on Social Media:

Linkedin - https://www.linkedin.com/in/thenewfuturist/

Facebook - https://business.facebook.com/thenewfuturist

Twitter - https://twitter.com/newfuturists

If you want to go EVEN FURTHER in driving and shaping the future, then The Foresight Academy is for YOU!

To find out more about "The Foresight Academy," and obtaining an official Certificate in Strategic Foresight from, Haslam College of Business, University of Tennessee, please visit: www.theforesightacademy.com

Journal:

_____

_____

_____

_____

_____

_____

_____

_____

_____

_____

_____

_____

_____

_____

_____

_____

_____

Made in the USA
San Bernardino, CA
19 October 2018